There's Fruit on me!

Written by Shaun Shirley
Illustrated by Brianna Scott

"...The fruit of the Spirit is love, Joy, peace, patience, kindness, goodness, gentleness, faithfulness, self-control."

Galatians 5:22-23

I'm like a tree,
I'm like a tree

that the
Lord
is good!

He's given me
LOVE
like Jesus

He's given me
JOY
that frees us

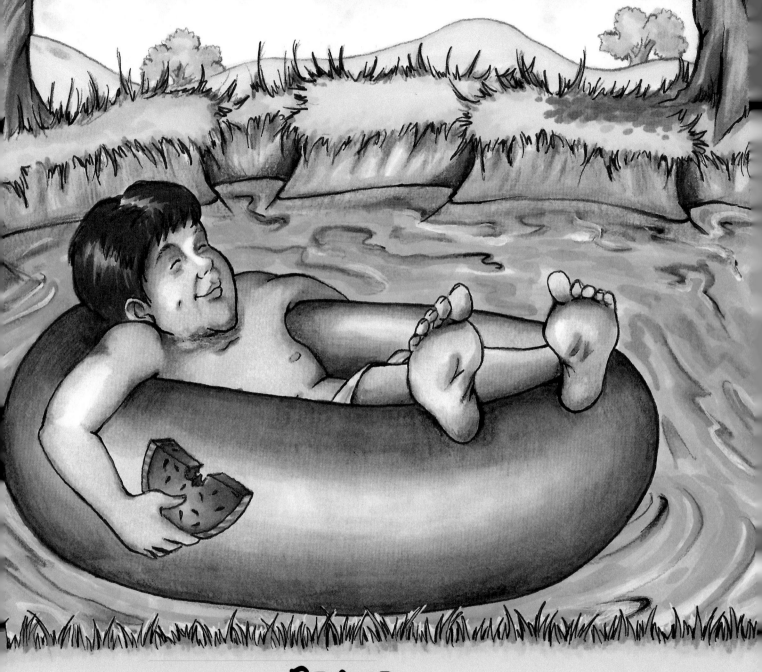

He's given me **PEACE** to calm the raging sea

He's given me PATIENCE

So I can wait there's no need for me to hesitate...

There's fruit on me!

GENTLENESS to mend
the broken wing

and
FAITHFULNESS
is on my tree

on my
very best day,
on my
very best day,
I'm
in control
of me

I'm like a tree, I'm like a tree,
He's put His Fruit all over me
come taste and see that the
Lord is Good!

There's **FRUIT** on me!

about the author
Shaun Shirley

Shaun Shirley, worship pastor for Children's Ministry at Bethel Church (Redding, Calfornia), received a gift of music at 16, and has been singing and song-writing ever since. Along with this gift, is a passion to lead people of all ages into the presence of God. Additionally, Shaun has a desire to transfer the truths she has gained in spending years worshipping with children into books for children of all ages.

Shaun has been married to Dake for over 26 years and is a mother of three children. Together they live in Redding and are part of Bethel's growing community.

Would you like the song and music that created this story?

There is music available that accompanies this book. If you would like to sing along, you can scan the code and purchase Shaun's ep that includes this and two more of her songs...

There's Fruit on me

(capo 3)

          G   D   EM   C2

I'm like a tree, I'm like a tree. He's put His fruit all over me

                        G   D   C2

Come taste and see that the Lord is good

(Repeat)

                 G   D

He's given me love like Jesus, He's given me joy that frees us

        EM   C2   G

He's given me peace to calm the raging sea He's given me patience, so

                     D

I can wait. There's no need for me to hesitate

        EM   C2   G

He's given me kindness to be who I ought to be. There's fruit on me. . .

Chorus

                   G

He's given me goodness to do the right thing

      D   EM   C2

And Gentleness to mend the broken wing. And faithfulness is on my tree

          G   D   EM   C2

On my very best day, on my very best day, I'm in control of me

Bridge

                          G

He's given me love and joy and peace and patience,

D   EM   C2

kindness, goodness, gentleness, And faithfulness, and self-control

(Repeat 3 x's)

                  G   D   EM   C2

I'm like a tree, I'm like a tree. He's put His fruit all over me

                       G   D   C2

Come taste and see that the Lord is good

                       G   D   C2

Come taste and see that the Lord is good

              D   G

There's fruit on me. . .

Also Available from Shaun Shirley...

Children's Worship Songs & Hand Motions Tutorial

There are hand motions available that go with this book! These tutorials include the music, chord charts, and videos of the hand motions.

Each volume contains 5 songs, you can scan the code below to learn more or to purchase...

¡Hay Fruto en Mí!

There's Fruit On Me! is now also available in Spanish!

You can scan the code below to purchase...

Don't feel like scanning a code? You can find all of Shaun Shirley's songs, hand motions, and books at:

www.shop.ibethel.org

53336618R00015

Made in the USA
Middletown, DE
27 November 2017